Enveiling

Andrys Onsman

Enveiling
and surrounding poems

Acknowledgements

Some of these poems have appeared previously (often in quite different versions) in *Island, Press Press, Perimeter* and other magazines, and on various electronic sites.

For Anne

Enveiling and surrounding poems
ISBN 978 1 76109 225 1
Copyright © Andrys Onsman 2021

First published 2021 by
GINNINDERRA PRESS
PO Box 3461 Port Adelaide 5015
www.ginninderrapress.com.au

Contents

A Brief History of Time	7
You See Everything in a Dream!	9
Parabolic	10
Father	11
Jochum Straatsma is Dead	12
Mother	13
Taking Turns	14
Precision	15
Enveiling	16
The Magi Came From the East	18
The Two Perspectives of Eden	19
Dendrochronology	20
Osprey	21
Toronto: from the outside	22
kunyani: Aurora Australis	23
Neptune's Mares	25
Zeus and Athena	26
Narcissus and Echo	27
Ariadne's Bargain	29
Penelope	34
The Song of the Sirens 2016	36
Icarus Gone	40
Eagle	42
Medusa	43
Cat	44
Brolga Dreaming	45
In Besozzo	46
Beached Whale	48
Crossing the Corpus Callosum	49
Marilyn's Corset	51

Every wave	53
Tasman's Bridge	54
Parlour Games	55
Imagining Janus	56
Self-discovery	57
Rembrandt's Diary	58
Spider Fingers	59
Bushfire	60
Gallery	61
Regarding the World From the Water	62
South Melbourne Beach at Dusk	63
Sea Horses	64
Exogeneity	65

A Brief History of Time

My grandfather's clock hangs
silently on the lounge room wall.
Relieved from keeping order,
it now records a deeper time.

I recall the man himself,
in rough serge pants held up
with a brown leather belt
and a blue peaked sailor's cap
though he'd never been to sea,
a man whose fortune lay in plans
and in nothing that he owned,
would take the butterfly key from
the battered brass tobacco tin
on the mantelpiece and,
as steadily as if he were in control
of the time being set,
rewind the clockworks' springs.

All for nought:
He's gone to dust.
Below the face,
behind the glass,
the pendulum
hangs still,
the disc a dull,
immobile sun,
the butterfly
discarded in
the old brass tin
collecting dust
on the shelf
beneath.

You See Everything in a Dream!

Let me sing you this song.
It doesn't hurt to listen once in a while to
blues sung with a battered voice, or
jazz sung through choking smoke, or
country with another man's torch and twang, or
amphetamine beats under the chorus
of an obvious truth caught in a single word.

'You see everything in a dream!'

So? Dreaming's all I know: my world
is my dream, my dream is my world,
the world of a big messy girl.

And in my dream I sing
and dance
and respond to skin
and look for spasms in my soul
(if my soul is in my guts).

And in my world I dream.

In the real world I look for voices
that I can speak with and
sing with,
take praise for and
wrap myself up in and
sometimes hide myself in.

I dream everything I see,
I hear everything I am.

Parabolic

for Ruben

The triumph of your arrival was relayed to me
Through a digitised text on my mobile phone

(A series of zeros and ones: nothings and beings;
Sartre made manifest in cyber space)

That triggered immediate action, a hurried haj to see
And assimilate your being alive through a fearful touch.

We all moved along a place when you came,
Leaving the skin of who we were behind where we sat.

The way of things is ebbs and flows, for which
We spend a lifetime fabricating memories,

Scratching names into stone, leaving our prints
For posterity: as if it matters beyond the here and now.

Our brains make meaning but our souls demand
That someone recognises our trajectory as a life,

That someone says, 'I knew that man alive. I touched
His paper skin. I am of him. I wept at his passing.'

A bell-curved arc from not yet to gone is
A metaphor for itself, a rising falling parable.

Father

To watch my father climb on ladders leant
against the walls of houses, shouldering
enormous rolls of asphalt and smouldering
pots of tar in masculine ascent,

was nothing short of watching death defied.
My childhood climbs a step or two and feels
the rungs have caught the rhythm of his heels,
and clings. The movement leaves me petrified.

The fear of falling keeps me from the skies.
At heights above my body's length a roar
of blood will rush into my ears before
a dazzling light explodes behind my eyes.

I crane my neck to see my father stand
beyond my reach. I'd fly to touch his hand.

Jochum Straatsma is Dead

Jochum Straatsma is dead. His body lies
Protected, hidden from view in a wooden box
Arthritis, gravity and the weight of the past
Had made him bend into a foetal curl.
Towards the end, if he managed to speak
His children couldn't understand the words.
They called him Dad; the neighbours called him Jack
And Jochum wondered where his name had gone.

Old Jochum Straatsma was my father's friend.
It was he who made my father old. White haired,
They talked of 'home' and 'here'; two places that
Could never be the same, for home was half
a world away and too many years ago,
and here had no real place or time for them.

Mother

The scales that measure what is in the heart
are calibrated with platitudes and guesswork,
and weighted with an irrational fear of forgiving
in others what might be found in our own.

There is a rhythm that exists without a beat.
The seasons come and go despite their names.
If winter were called spring it would still be cold;
The sky would still be crisply blue and dry.

The imperfect tides drag and wash, scrape
And batter the land without desire or will.
They simply come and go, while we assign them
Words like Grace and God and fate and fear.

The time from conception to birth is set
Regardless of how we partition it.
A spinning dial doesn't measure time – it
Names it. We shall call this block an hour.

I'll pass it on. You are of me and I'm of her,
Like frames of time, markers of partitioning.
This is mine, a light switched on, waiting to be
Doused, aflame for long enough to light the way.

Taking Turns

for Anne

I like the imprint of breasts and belly,
Of skin flattened and wet on my thigh,
The twist of your hip when you fall away.

I like the sun-trapped tangle of hair that
Defies your ears to fall around your face
And spider-walk on my skin as you turn.

I like that your eyes are open as you create
A story that has no life beyond its telling,
A memory shared without forward thought.

I like the smell of your skin as you talk.
I listen to the tale, embrace its unfolding,
The improvised theatre of catch and release.

Precision

Listen – at first to nothing.
The silence wraps around
the essence of life like
the dark around a candle.

From the common soul
a rhythm is drawn to the light,
an iambic beat, alive
in water, a mirrored pulse.

A heart gathers strength.
A wound-up spring that
sets time in motion
as it starts to unwind

and nothing will stop it
until an accepted death:
nothing in life can stop
the construct of time.

The heartbeat is relentless:
it has no human syllable:
uncoiling, discharging
energy until the time

you stop to listen, and no
longer hear the echo.
And then in the silence
the pulse dissolves again.

Enveiling

for Ynys

The midnight bus, a silver spool that
Reels in the thread of the miles of road
Between the city of churches and my heart,
Draws me, drowsily awake, back to you.

In the seats across the aisle, an old lady sleeps,
Her head against the bag against the window,
Her jaw slack, sinking into her chin, into her coat,
Twisting as if she is used to turning in her bed.

The bus is cheap. With neither speed
Nor romance, it carts the poor and dispossessed
From one situation to another with hope,
Like a lottery ticket bought with change.

The man in front of me is nodding to
Whatever is playing in his headphones.
Reflected in the window I see a glimpse
Of unkempt hair, a tear tattoo, closed eyes.

Whether arriving or receiving, we
Are moving differently over common ground.
Memories, the building blocks of relationships,
Take time to recall, and first they must be made.

In the angled mirror above the driver's seat
A slash of face, scowling in concentration,
Is focused on the arc of light ahead of the bus,
The headlights approaching, the darkness.

I hunker down, close my eyes and listen
To the hum of the fidget wheels. In this capsule,
the world is defined: a set time, a limited space.
You are my purpose beyond the here and now.

The Magi Came From the East

It was neither a year nor a meaningful time:
Simply a tick of the nuclear clock.
Stars were stars: they were neither codes
Nor predictors of fortune and fate.

To underline the legend with science,
Carbon-dating and probability scans suggest
That it wasn't nearly as bad as a barn or a stable:
More like a cellar for rent, a cheap B&B.

Not that it matters if he were born at all:
The magi had come bearing gifts for a god
And a god would be found regardless of time.
The gifts were unloaded with faith and relief,

And accepted without favour or fear,
As children do. Gold, myrrh and frankincense
Well past their due date but heartfelt no less,
Things we'd have given, had we given Him things.

The Two Perspectives of Eden

From the front, a garden spins in patterns
Predictable as plans. The plants are trimmed
And pruned, the colours manicured and edged.
With pesticide and diligence, each branch
Becomes a frame for every leaf and blade,
And every day a call to recommit.

Coming in the back, the garden unfolds
And demands a new interpretation,
A shedding of clothes. Remember how we
Came dressed to the hilt in thick winter wear,
Discarding each garment as we walked through
The long wet grass and unkempt orchard trees,
Revelling in how every path presented
A surprising new perspective?

Dendrochronology

Melbourne is a zonal town. The chronology
of émigrés is written in the rings of urban sprawl.
First, a flex of muscle and gun claimed the land and
rammed a beachhead into the cradle of the bay,

and then the usurpers wiped it clean, preparing it
for others from abroad who, inspected and judged worthy,
were made welcome to transplant their philosophies.
And we came in waves on ocean-crossing steel sarcophagi.

At Station Pier the names of the immigrant ships
are carved, without a hint of irony, onto the bow
of a sculpted wreck. Perhaps the artist thought that we,
the new arrivals, had left our pasts on board.

In truth, those memories crowded out everything else
that we had crammed into our tattered bags, and
as soon as we found a place in our allotted suburb
we planted them like seeds in the gardens of this town,

where they bloom, beautiful foreign hues and shapes
to remind us that we are not where we were; that home,
though now much closer than it was, is somewhere else
and we, like hermit crabs, are anchored foreigners.

Osprey

The ocean seldom provides an easy feast.

On the cliff face, an osprey hunches
his shoulders tucked in like a gargoyle,
watching the water, judging the odds.

There are no thoughts that he pursues
as he launches his will into space,
to fall on the shivering waves below.

Looking elsewhere, he swoops,
dragging his talons like grappling irons,
to snatch and rise above the turmoil

with the world hanging onto his feet.

Toronto: from the outside

The third hour of the new year,
Toronto sleeps under a quilt
Of freshly fallen snow.
The hotel room has drawn in,

Like the cell of a monk or a thief.
A dry dusty heat comes from a box
That purrs like a cat on the wall
But does nothing for the soul.

This frontier town is clean
But underneath the grid of streets
Lie labyrinthine catacombs,
Skinner boxes without reward.

At midnight, we emerged to shout
And blast the old year's ghosts away.
Drunk and fearless of the cold, we
Dragged new hope into the underground.

kunyani: Aurora Australis

A monolithic thrust of hard
plutonic rock defies the cold
Antarctic sea. Its craggy tor
is polar whipped by freezing winds.

A road has scarred the mountain with
its scything cuts. The humbled rock
now lurches, broken-backed – a giant
brooding lump of beaten black.

The shafts of light that slash the night
in arcs describe a slow ascent.
The driver's eyes are hard. His face
is thin, the skin is taut on bones.

A pulse ago, a sign of light
was sent towards the moving man.
Vibrations race in angled waves
of cranked-up ions, standing still.

Such independent movement is
the purest form of energy
for solar winds are purposeless
beyond the Earth's ionosphere.

In perfect black, the sky at night,
electric radiation from
the southern pole's magnetic grasp
is hung in brilliant fans of green

and powdered with a touch of red.
This hologram of incoherent light
is far too big, too filled with awe
to entertain the petty fears

that drove the man so close to God.
There is no room beyond the place
assigned: the sky protects the man
like skin against the wind and cold:

the pulse of life laid bare. The tears
that catch the light are for the vast
display of pyrotechnic grace.
The sun at night defies the heart.

Neptune's Mares

I bring you horses, Cormac, strong and fleet
of foot, with wild and unforgiving eyes
and flaring nostrils, snorting to the beat
of freedom pumping blood into the heart.

When rains fall hard, you'll hear the hurtling hoofs
of Spirit Horses running thunder skies
on legs that rock the trees and trample roofs
and, having come, are eager to depart

for Neptune's mares: the mob of water beasts
who race beneath the waves. You'll see their heads
appear on windswept seas, the promised feasts,
the call to love on swaying silken beds.

And when the horses call for you, be brave
And take the chance to ride a tiding wave.

Zeus and Athena

You were my dream. I made you in my head.
No intertwining of genetic code,
you were new and perfect, conceived to be
everything I want in a father's child.
The difference between being made and bred
is the chance of a hiccup at the next crossroad.
The wisdom comes from your mother, still in me,
and through her, the human factor's reconciled.

More than beauty I made you wise and strong:
those long lean limbs can carry the world,
when the world goes wrong. It's all in the mind.
Talk to me, tell me your story, sing me your song,
Show me where in the wind your words have swirled.
This headache is the space you left behind.

Narcissus and Echo

Utterly self-absorbed. To gaze into a mirror and see
Nothing but the image of myself, and fall desperately in love.
Away from the glass I can still smell your perfumed skin
And recall the gasp as your bare shoulder catches my breath.

Having struggled through and after the nightmare,
The jungles of doubt and self-delusional grandeur
Half demented, entirely beyond the pale until morning,
Staggering to the promise of relief in a still water pond

To slake an unforgiving thirst and, falling to my knees,
To drink the darkness away. And there and then I saw
Myself: a ragged dirty man, so full of deceitful grace, a man
To love, and saw myself as my brother, my lover, my life.

You, a shadow brushing against the skin in the past,
A convex surface that reflects my body but not my soul,
Are exclusive, nothing beyond the limbs and flesh, even
As I fall into your embrace again. You are me, only me,

Compulsive self-obsession, a text-booked syndrome
Responsive to treatment and prescribed pharmacopeia
But the will to repent is an unlikely cure. It's not the vain
Who are at fault but those who agree. And I drink to slake.

Now you are gone, I hear your voice, as clear as a bell
And each wave of sounds hangs heavily on my shoulders.
Like the purpose of a breeze through the mountains,
it's my name that floats, the breath of me, my cure of you.

Uncontested vanity loses its venom. Like an opiate,
a comparison loses its sting when the result is already known.
Sweet Echo, this is my punishment: to know that I am
Beautiful and that every whisper is a reminder of the lost you.

Ariadne's Bargain

I

Like surplus, the island hangs beneath the continental mass, discarded and removed. The people who live there are either refuse caught on the wrong side of partition or shipwrecked flotsam who drifted ashore on currents that swirled them away from the main.

High up in the middle of the island, under a bone-achingly cold curtain of mist and rain, a wild confusion of indistinguishable tarns and ridges forms an unforgiving labyrinth. And the beast in the heart of the living maze is fed by the broken bodies and battered souls of those who dared to enter. Each year here a heart is sacrificed even though there's nothing to be forgiven and no god to be appeased.

In the labyrinth we lose our sense of self, the mental map of who we are. We are stripped of present time, each moment no more than a fleeting instant press-ganged between what we have been and what we could be. The past and the future have intent and purpose but the present is pointless, gone as soon as it's found, like God, like Boson-Higgs, like love.

II

Having been chosen, Theseus is reluctant. To enter is suicide. To refuse is suicide too, for cowardice is punished by death. The old men – that they are old is testament to the luck of the draw – manhandle him to edge of the veil, and having pointed to the way in, leave. Under the double-edged sword hanging by a thread over his head, Theseus stands still, unable to move forward, unable to move back. To be a hero he can't stay where he is and bereft of other options he decides that bravery at least will emblazon his name. But for the moment he is unwilling.

III

Then, a voice from the liminal edge beckons him. A woman, barely that, a girl, doe-like, copper toned and small, shy but sure and at home in the present, calls him and having no other options, he moves towards her.

She sings her song like a bellbird.

This is my labyrinth.
I spun the web around the beast
I have kept the thread.
I know how to beat the fear.

To find your way, I'll give you the past;
To kill the beast, the here and now;
To get out free, the promise of the new.

And all of these I'll give to you
If in return you give yourself to me.
Should you want to give yourself to me.

Enabled by her words and wisdom, he enters and kills and having wiped the blood from his sword, follows the thread back to where the bargain was made.

IV

Promises sworn at death's door are readily made and therefore brittle and easily broken. Within the blink of an eye Ariadne grew into a woman at the centre of a web. The bargain, though honestly struck, cancered into a deceitful ruse, and her love became possessive, a leash, a limit, a shackle he needed to break. Ariadne knew that having killed the beast in the labyrinth, Theseus had always been free to go. And so, led by the long-limbed Athena, he left, cocksure and smug, as ever unaware of what he was to her.

V

We exile vanquished foes and past mistakes,
the godless heretics, the lunatics,
unsightly lepers, children misconceived,
or anyone we need to keep at bay,
to barren isles: as if beyond the sea
is far enough away. This island swarms
with life; its hinterland's a labyrinth,
a maze of pathways blocked at every turn.

As Ariadne watched her lover's ship
sail past the line between the sea and sky
she ached without remorse and yearned to feel
his breath, his skin on hers, the him-in-her.
Her story is a yarn that's spun like threads
of DNA into our common heart.

Penelope

Half a breath away from widowhood,
Youth plundered by your absence, I have
Become a woman of a certain age. I am
No goddess, no stoic heroine at her loom.
Every day another suitor comes,
Not for who I am but for what I am thought to be.
Rumours of your return mean nothing to them now
And my virtue has become my own concern.
You on the sea-road were free to ransack
While I was hamstrung by your child
And by vows made to you and by responsibility
And by consignment to a minor role.

In the past few years I seldom thought of you
And when I did, I had no inclination to be kind.
Your great adventure has taken everything
From me when I was a part of us.
With your parting kiss you sucked the life out of me,
Just as your men, your boon companions,
The husbands and lovers of women and men
Took all that they could carry when they left.

And let's be honest here. You assumed that
Your heroic undertakings would make you a god
Or at least a demigod, more than just a legend.
You were so sure the Fates would grant you that.

It is difficult, now, to welcome you back to the isle
Where the labyrinth and I are not what we were.
Under the tattered sails I see worn-out men,
Delirious, with long and greying beards.
Oh, I no longer have need of men and you,
My once-husband, are obviously no god. I need
My sisters' wings and a clear path between
The sun and the sea.

The Song of the Sirens 2016

In post-apocalypse Paris the sirens sing out
Two-tone cries for mercy. Cobblestones,
Bloodied by past demands, glow softly
Under ornate, twisted street lamps.
On the arrow-straight avenues that link
The regulate circles of honour into a web,
Taxis hurtle like pinballs from door to door.
At night, the city keeps its lights on,
Its eyes open and its ears to the ground.
The citizens now are afraid of shadows.

The daily displays of defiance by those
Who stand as one with the innocent accused
Are protected by the gendarmerie that allows people
To protest in safety. But with the darkness
Comes uncertainty and no one marches at night.

Not all of the accused are innocent.
The quire of willing helpers who take
No responsibility for the murders,
The mayhem, the mangled aftermath
Caused by the arrows they protect,
Claim to be common folk who
Chat to ordinary neighbours,
Raise children attending local schools
And playing in parks with others like them,
Somehow find a way to turn
A blind eye to the carnage caused
By the missiles they've hidden,
Arrows shot for maximum effect.

It defies both logic and belief.
Those who protect the archers
Have neither claim to afterlife
Nor comfort in the present.
Most know this is not the will of God:
The women who parked a car primed
To explode outside the Notre Dame
Were exposed as killers by their father;
A man who saved the lives of many
At the expense of his own.

A block away on Rue Saint Denis,
The whores who need to eat
Lean against the grilled shop doors
And watch like vipers as I walk past,
Ready to strike should a glance
In their direction warrant the work.

And then on barred and
Barricaded Rue Sebastopol,
I'm tied to the mast like a target.
The boulevard is straight but empty
Even though it's nigh on time to eat.
I can taste the fear, bitter in the mouth,
In this ordinary evening.
A convoy comes: armour-plated,
Black with tinted windows, limousines
Driven by stern-faced men.

Moving in precision towards the Arc
De Triomphe. The sirens' song
Bounces off the glass and brick
Walls of the canyon like a
Fusillade. I imagine the guards
Sitting inside like Ulysses' men
Are watching me watching them.

With my companions safely out of earshot
I mimic the siren's call; sing a little song
To pitch the notes. Goodbye, goodbye.
God be with you. God be with you
As their God is with them. Scylla and
Charybdis; a rock and hard place;
On Earth as it is in Heaven.

Like a flapping bat above me, a chopper
Rotor blades through the heavy air
At the end of this dank and dismal day.

For a while I stand and wait
And watch but nothing stirs
Until a motorcycle speeds
Towards me as if cannon-shot.
The rider sits crouched low,
wrapped around the machine
Head hung low, maybe simply
enjoying the freedom or maybe
something else. I step back, closer
To the wall and wait until he races past,
Alarmed as the matt black helmet
Turns to keep an eye on me.

I pray this mast is stronger than my fear,
stronger than the siren's call, and
stronger than the motorcycle's roar.

Paris, my oldest love, my go-to place,
Whose arteries are as bruised as mine,
Is waiting for Orpheus to retune his lyre.
His music is stronger than the sirens that
Scream their song into the night
But for now his voice is hoarse
And the underground has seeped up
Onto the cobbled streets like a shroud

And the Sirens sing their warning song.

Icarus Gone

Imagine the joy of being released
From the pull of the Earth, the thrill of a
Cartwheel without gravity to suck
The freedom out of the movement
And drag us back into the labyrinth.

With Icarus in his slipstream,
Daedalus had broken out of the maze.
But when he turned mid-flight to share
The joy of escape with his only son,
There was no one in an empty sky.

Immobile and struck dumb by incredulity,
Daedalus hangs Heaven-high
With slowly beating, giant wings
Eddying the air into whirlpools and
Keeping him aloft without a cause.

Then comes the howl of recognition.
Beneath him, feathers drift like flowers
On the surface of water, like a scattered circle
Of prayer for the dead and a message:
You have ventured where no man may go.

The trespass was not daring to flee but
Daring to fly, and by disrupting the order
Of things, to create an inheritance
That defies the law of natural science.
If this, then how will gods be set apart?

Having been done, it can't be undone but a life
Without issue has made it done in vain.
Daedalus hangs forever crucified in the air
Between the sun and rolling sea below.

Eagle

With shoulders hunched, a dust brown eagle
rests, self-contained, on the highest branch.
The gun-turret head is perfectly still.
The sun explodes its lidless eyes.

He marks the terrain below with a cross
and examines each quarter for movement.
From this height, the world is a relief
of living things in perfect detail.

You will not feel the shadow of his gaze
when his sinews tighten with harsh intent
but the angle of his head has fallen cruel

You may, if you are quick, be aware of
a sudden gust of air as he falls on you,
clamps you and carries you up to heaven.

Medusa

The ocean here is teeming
And it breaks a million hearts.

A barely-there Medusa
drifts above me,
billowing, translucent,
pulsating, watching,
living mute, unflinching,
like an abandoned bride,
a woman scorned,
with the devil
on a trailing thread.

The ocean lives. It is the
perfect place for heartache.

Cat

The mid-stretch death
Has left one paw extended
Like swimmer, mid-stroke,
Frozen at the turn, until

The lazy curl to foetus and
Opening his ruffled frill
To trap the morning sun.

In the square of sunlight
Warming the feathers on the bed
The flick of his tail warns of
His sensual dangerous strength.

He's clean, smoky grey and white,
And moves with an African beat
In the shadows of his forbears.

Brolga Dreaming

At the forkstick entrance I lie coiled,
waiting for the thunder to run along the
bottom of the gathering clouds.

Then you dance me on stilted legs and beckon
me with swaying wings, lift me, uncurl me
and dream me into the long grass.

Before the thunder of the gathering clouds
ripples dance across the hidden water place
behind the forkstick entrance.

We fall into the long deserted place,
the other world of movement and dream
away from the gathering thunder clouds.

Our tongues twist into one another and
we move, swaying in the rising wind,
inside the open water place

and leave subtle marks of movement and
dreams in the long grass where we lie,
waiting for the clouds from the west.

In Besozzo

the night controls the vision of the heart.

It might be said, if one were asked,
that the tiny heart of the town beats
rapidly like a newborn baby bird –
but that would be a flattering lie.
Besozzo's heart is nervous like
the pulse of the matron, white and frail,
hunched up in a favourite chair,
waiting for the call to let it go.

Outside the ochre walls of ancient houses
on trails of footpath that stop and start,
pompous boys and girls stand in surly pairs
wearing leather clothes and teased up hair
anticipating action (as youth wait
everywhere, for anything to fill the void,
the lack of promise that hangs like mist
in every country town around the world).

Nothing comes except the angled man
who scowls his way towards the outside world
that lies beyond the telephone line
with twice as many numbers as a local call.
He starts the conversation with a grunt
then vaguely smiles at the reflection
that bounces off the glass protection
that keeps Besozzo from the man.

At night this crowd of history in stone
(the old church frescoed in a fading faith;
the hilltop beacon to the wartime dead;
the orange light that smooths the ragged walls
of streets with shadows darker than the night;
the verdant damp of rotting plants:
the obverse of the summer's brightest colours)
swirls around the ragazzi like a cloak.
They pin their faith and money on their Vespas
that rev up like mosquitoes' battle cries.

But there can be no light, no noise, no curse,
no will that could ever overcome the weight
of nights like this, dumped on small Italian towns
and through which I push my way back home
when all the coins I had have gone,
aware that as I breathe this thick air in

Besozzo breathes it out.

Beached Whale

So very hot! The water turns to mist
And disappears like Soul to Universe.
My skin is blistered, dry and cancer-kissed.

I have no regrets about this last embrace.
The strength of instinct is a powerful force.
And freedom is an act of simple grace.

She sings to me, a water-bearing nurse,
When pouring buckets of water over my face.
Caressing my skin she whispers tender words

Because there is no way back from here.
She lives and breathes and needs to stay alive
But I, though of this place, have no such fears.

The energy that makes my bones, my heart
Will dissipate into the universal soul, provide
The next in line with building blocks to start

Anew somewhere, a different form of life
Perhaps, with no recall of mine. Her tears
Are salt, and dissipate into the ebbing tide

Crossing the Corpus Callosum

For the initial surprise explosion
On the freewheeling side of my brain,
The side where excitement abounds
And everything is possible, the puppy dog
Side, the toddling wide-eyed side, to move

To the side of detail, of things made small
And minutely examined, carefully considered,
Balanced, tested, abstracted, contained, made
To fit with what is there and stored for recall,
It has to cross the *corpus callosum*

The nerves that guard against excess.
Seen from above, the *corpus callosum*
Is a hide, pegged out for drying in the sun
Waiting to become leather, a butterfly flap
That traps ideas like Venus and her flies.

Besieged into submission by the limbic
Machine, ideas that cross the *corpus callosum*
Are bridled and contained like photographs
Of strangers, to be regarded rather than relived,
And once on the other side, are unable to return.

Except for love, all love. Despite the Hippo
Campus, Amygdala, the basal bits and bobs,
Love defies the trap and swings from side to side
Like Janus on the turps. Blithely indifferent
Or cocking a snoot, love remains a tidal spread

That ebbs and floods, renews and re-excites
The ganglia, the optic thingamajig, and, oh yes,
The ilioinguinal nerves, always those, a mind
Of their own, when a shoulder is bared, a smile
Is shared, a move is made, a bridge is crossed.

Marilyn's Corset

Everyone knows that idiots tell the finest tales
when they forget that they're acting on a stage;
when the sound and the fury, the signified nothing
is their own. They strut and fret, swing and
sway, and shout at the shadows on the periphery.
Not being heard is a minor inconvenience;
much less of a blow than no longer bellowing
in rage against the world outside the window
or laughing at the madness inside the room.

So, let's talk about the hour then. Neither fixed
nor free, it stretches or contracts according to
what's crammed into its compass. The speed
at which the sand drips through Miss Monroe's
waist depends upon the thickness of the grains.
And if a whole world rests within each single one
and if each hour holds infinity, there's time enough
for fools to rush, scattering angels like nine-pins
and breaching the wall of twittering seraphim
who stand undecided and afraid to reach beyond
their grasp. The headline cast are unconcerned
that they will not be heard once off this mortal coil.
The praises and the pity of others are of no concern
to fools. Their tales are not told for a magistrate's
bench, or a hand-clapping pew of converts, riveted
to their seats like trespassers to their stocks.
Theirs are the tales that exist simply in the telling.

All puffery, of course, mere cant, and despair:
The longest night turns us all into madmen and fools.
When the candle's snuffed and the hereafter is here
and now, the stage will be re-dressed and painted anew,
and crowded with poor players poised to sing the script
again. We all are pinched tightly at the waist.

Every wave

Every wave is perfect and unique:
There is no standard, there is no norm.

From the tiny ripple that plays
With the dancing toes of children

To the smashing rampage of
An earthquaking wall of power,

Every wave has a single cause
A shift in place, a seismic thrust

And it flows over oceans of time
Building potential, displacing force

And if left unattended, it fades back
To nothing, a perfect singular event

That in an instant changed the world.

Tasman's Bridge

A whirling knot of starlings unties
to thread itself through the pylons of the bridge
while a goshawk circles innocently above.

I'm caught between the hunter and its prey,
of no benefit to either; here to scan horizons
and contemplate what lies beyond.

I stop at the highest point of its arching back
without the urge to test my base resolve,
content to tread water in the here and now.

This is my bridge; this skyscraping concrete span
made unsafe by the first fall into the oblivion
of the gun-barrel-grey water below.

Years ago, a ship drifted against a midstream leg
and the span crashed onto its bow. Cars sailed into space
then disappeared in the blackness below. People died.

The captain, drunk, asleep, was doomed to survive
and live for a while as a ghost. The city, divided again,
rained curses on him and learned to live as siblings.

The years it took to fix were trying. The separated banks
grew apart and incompetence denied a seamless repair,
its elegance sacrificed to the need to reconnect.

No longer perfect but functional, I barely see its faults.
It brings salvation because although I've never been sailor,
I've learnt to stay sober at the helm.

Parlour Games

The spider's web is two-dimensional.
To overcome unequal shape, she anchors
Long diagonals across an open space
That cross at the point of origin of a perfectly

Coordinated Cartesian plane; a silken
Thin Saint Andrew's cross, held in place
By a bridge line spanning the abyss
At its highest point. From within the centre

She uses the full extent of her limber legs
To measure the length of each hub, the spokes
Of the web, spinning careful radii
Of entrapment with the finest of lace.

In a certain light, say early morning mist or
At the end of those days when the sun takes an age
To set, the threads are luminescent white
Against a swathe of shades of dark portent.

She waits in the heart of the shimmering world,
Feeling the tension of every string she's ready
To pull. The weaver has but one design: to snare
The unsuspecting innocents who dare to fly.

This is her corridor; you will not pass through.
There is no argument, no clemency to beg for.
Once caught, your angel wings are of no avail
And she, a careful acrobat, will eat you alive.

Imagining Janus

for Alex Selenitsch

The world is built on hypotheses and
Propositions, the yin and yang of
Old hat and not yet known, the dragons'
Fight beneath an edifice of truth.
Janus, the liminal god, is damned
To see both sides of the argument
And entertain all ambiguities,
Caught fast between the now of yes and no.

As one face is drawn to the future
And the other's dragged back by the past
He's coolly even-handed (when being fair
Is seldom the best response) simply
Because he has no shoulder to shrug
To justify the choice he would have made.

Self-discovery

He paints the cosmic thrum that rules the tide
of human life. The webs of his untidy spi-
der catch the fears before there's time to hide
behind the order of the artist's eye.
He died before analysis: his art
remains a testament, the perfect foil –
despite our need to understand his part
in terms of fixed ideas of honest toil.

The lines are space designs of perfect or-
der; nothing overblown, precision marks
of self-control and self examina-
tion. Pollock guides the sand-blown lights and darks
of autumn's cycle far beyond the bor-
der of the work. He planned it that way.

Rembrandt's Diary

The empty space around his head is charged
With energy, a bed of silence loud
With nervous thought that waits to be enlarged
With reasoned dabs of paint. His face is proud
Enough to show the lines without disdain
And soft enough to capture distant views
Beyond what can be framed. Arthritic pain
Has put an end to artificial hues.

The easy portraits painted in his youth
Are full of room to move and time to grow.
His eyes as yet belie the basic truth
That art is driven by the need to know.
The space between his tired eyes and mine
Is caught along the horizontal line.

Spider Fingers

Even though you know full well he's peering
At his reflection just long enough to make
Another mark upon his canvassed self,
It seems as if he looking at your soul.

Relentless, hard, intense, his steady gaze
Will draw you in. You may avert your eyes
But Albrecht Dürer doesn't flinch. He stares
And though you look away, you're in his sights.

But look again. It's not his eyes. His art
Is in his hands. The thumb is pulled towards
The palm. The index finger, stroking fur
Is longer than a man's should be. The nail
Is polished, clean, unlike a painter's hand,
The nick beneath the knuckle long since healed.

Bushfire

Geoff Dyer (1947–2020)

Dyer pastes ribbons of paint on a sheet
Of canvas and fire bursts out, a roaring flame,
A twisting shaft of life-destroying heat
That reaches out beyond the painting's frame.
His art is to articulate the land ablaze;
The smell of burning bark, the ashen grey,
The begging for rain from a tight blue sky,
The cry to God from the black crows that fly
With heavy wings towards the glistening bay,
Where people stand in silent shallows, gaze
In disbelief at how their lives can turn,
How violently the quiet earth can burn.

And all of us who came to toast and praise
The man, are silenced by the memory.

Gallery

for Baukje Wytsma

Images, stripped back and bare, like a slashed wrist
Showing the bone that carries the flesh, a list
Of elements on display like an exhibition of dreams,
They mount like movie stills, each more than it seems
And the whole greater than the sum of the parts,
Smudged shots of time and space, of minds and hearts,
Of long forgotten ways of seeing the world, framed
So that the gaze will drift into what exists un-named.

In this gallery caught between two cardboard ends
Behind each word, the walls are white. The room lends
Itself to introspection, a shuffling progression past light
Thrown on canvas, a mummers' tale, the built delight
Of adding more upon more, each image new, each
A step towards the next, each a suture for the breach.

Regarding the World From the Water

Like clowns intent on drowning in our giant shoes
we wade backwards, singularly and apart,
through the gun-barrel water of Port Philip's bay
towards the line between the sea and sky.

When the water reaches a comfortable height
we stop and with arms crossed,
a child hoisted high on a hip because
we're far enough away, each an island.

Silent, mesmerised, we scan
(as if we know what we're looking for)
the shadows and lights of the hulking city,
held back from the beach by the esplanade.

The water lapping like a lover on my naked thighs,
the evening brushing cool against my cheek,
the sea breeze ruffling strands of hair, the separation,
all these caresses are beginning to be enough.

South Melbourne Beach at Dusk

A low-slung crescent moon
has slipped under the evening star
ready to catch it should it fall.
They have the sky to themselves
in these few moments between
day and night, when the horizon
is a band of orange light that brushes
up into the mid-blue vastness.

The people standing statue still
in the shallow waters of the bay
are silhouettes. Seabirds wheel
slowly, silently, like shadows
or souls seeking the gap between
this world and the next.

Sea Horses

Water must get between the rubber and the skin
for the body to stay warm in a wetsuit.

Paddling in the freezing water off Sorrento
I wait for my hands and feet to go numb.

I dive into the current that stirs the water
Around the rocks and let it carry me down.

Amongst the weeds float tiny sea horses,
the dragon-men of the infinite deep.

They hover fearlessly as I catch them
in the beam of my torch, and I am caught.

I want to show them that I know them,
but mine is silver-chained around my neck

whilst they float freely, untidily.
I watch them for the length of my air.

They watch me for longer. They watch me leave.
I have left no imprint anywhere.

Seahorses, dragon-men of the unknown:
the silver chain is my heart.

Exogeneity

Bleached bones trap a living space,
builds its form from inside out.

Unlike fossils, memories
vulcanised by gods of time,

this dragon's exo-skeleton
is armour-plated nothingness.

Seas deliver oddities;
shells and sponges, cuttlefish,

washed up spines and anchor-lines:
life-defining summaries,

Just containers, vacant homes,
empty vessels, perfect for

life above horizon skies.
Dreaming of depths, you whisper

'Take my empty seahorse shell,
fill it with your reckless heart.'

www.ingramcontent.com/pod-product-compliance
Lightning Source LLC
Chambersburg PA
CBHW062200100526
44589CB00014B/1882